FREEDOM TO EXPRESS YOURSELF

AN INSPIRATION NOTEBOOK

LOM ART

in association with Amnesty International UK

Edited by Sophie Schrey
and Imogen Williams
Designed by Zoe Bradley
and Jack Clucas
Cover design by Angie Allison
and Andrea D'Aquino

Cover artwork by
Mia Charro, Frances Ives,
Keith Negley, Hannah Rollings
and Lizzy Stewart

Every reasonable effort has been made to acknowledge
all copyright holders. Any errors or omissions that may
have occurred are inadvertent, and anyone with any
copyright queries is invited to write to the publishers,
so that a full acknowledgement may be included in
subsequent editions of this work.

First published in Great Britain in 2017 by LOM ART,
an imprint of Michael O'Mara Books Limited,
9 Lion Yard, Tremadoc Road, London SW4 7NQ

W www.mombooks.com
f Michael O'Mara Books
🐦 @OMaraBooks

A CIP catalogue record for this book is available from the British Library.

ISBN: 978-1-910552-54-4

2 4 6 8 10 9 7 5 3 1

This book was printed in China

A note from Amnesty

'Everyone has the right to freedom of expression and opinion'
Article 19, Universal Declaration of Human Rights

Many of us express ourselves as naturally as we breathe. We say what
we think, we write, paint, draw, make music. Our individual right to freedom
of expression is tempered only by the need to respect the rights of others.
Without Article 19 our lives would be immeasurably poorer.

But around the world artists, writers and activists are censored, often the
first to be targeted by repressive governments who fear the challenge of
words and art and the power of ideas to inspire change.

We hope the words and pictures in this notebook inspire you to draw, write and
doodle to your heart's content – to enjoy your right to freedom of expression.

We are grateful to all our contributing artists and writers. They belong
to a long and noble line of people who have stood up for truth, equality
and justice throughout history. Thank you.

A Famished Rd by Ben Okri

2 June 22

Magnificent imagination, soaked in humanity.

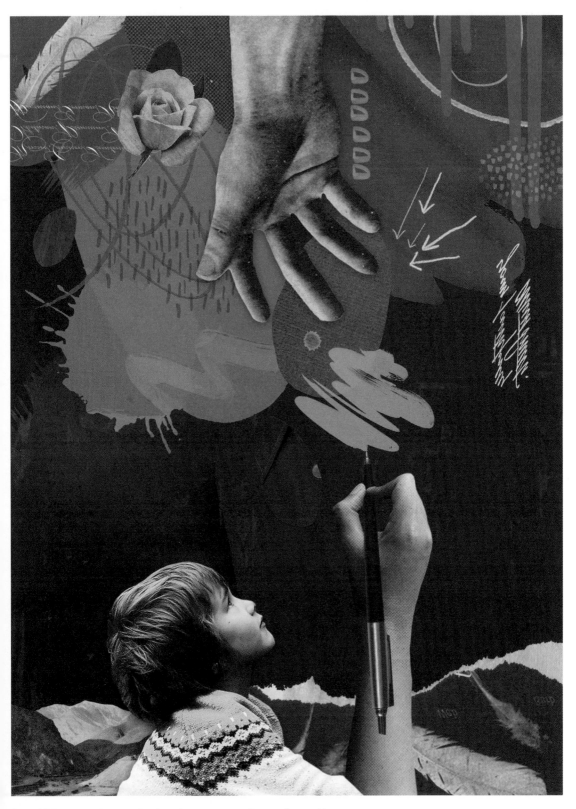

One child, one teacher, one book and one pen can change the world
Malala Yousafzai

Eleanor Shakespeare

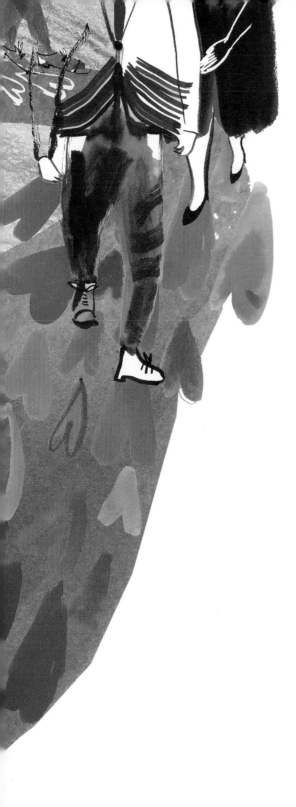

Darkness cannot put out darkness: only light can do that.
Hate cannot drive out hate: only love can do that.
Martin Luther King, Jr.

Hannah Rollings

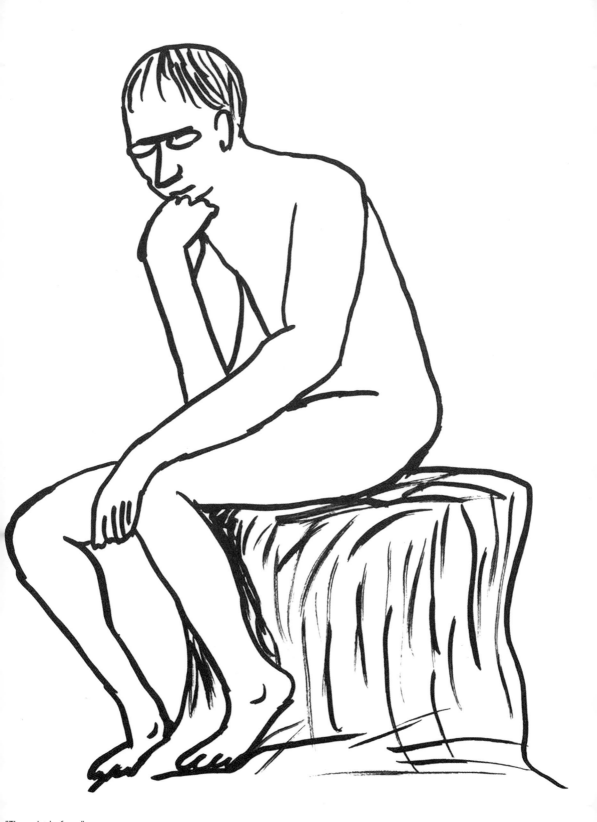

"Thought is free."
William Shakespeare, from *The Tempest*

David Shrigley

The land flourished because it was fed from so many sources – because it was nourished by so many cultures and traditions and peoples.
Lyndon B. Johnson

Mia Charro

The spoken words of an angel are clear to the touch in all ways... listen through your heart's meaning... listen close to the RHYTHM of the MotherLand...

What air is to the lungs, what light is to the eyes, what love is to the heart, liberty is to the soul of man.
Robert G. Ingersoll

Shane W. Evans

Reach me a gentian, give me a torch!
D. H. Lawrence, from 'Bavarian Gentians'

Natalie Hughes

Get up, stand up: stand up for your rights.
Get up, stand up: don't give up the fight.
Bob Marley, from 'Get Up, Stand Up'

Frances Ives

"I am no bird; and no net ensnares me;
I am a free human being with an independent will"
Charlotte Brontë, from *Jane Eyre*

Christopher Corr

"You have no mind to be unkind,"
    Said echo in her ear:
"No mind to bring a living thing
    To suffering or fear.
For all that's bad, or mean, or sad, you have no mind, my dear."
Lewis Carroll, from 'To Janet Merriman'

Wen Dee Tan

the Censor's sword pierces deeply into the heart of free expression

EARL WARREN

Ashley Le Quere

'Home', **Raouf Karray**

First they came for the Socialists, and I did not speak out — because I was not a Socialist.
Then they came for the Trade Unionists, and I did not speak out — because I was not a Trade Unionist.
Then they came for the Jews, and I did not speak out — because I was not a Jew.
Then they came for me, and there was no one left to speak for me.
Martin Niemöller

Hannah Rollings

YOU JUST HOLD YOUR HEAD HIGH AND KEEP THOSE FISTS DOWN. NO MATTER WHAT ANYBODY SAYS TO YOU, DON'T YOU LET 'EM GET YOUR GOAT. TRY FIGHTIN' WITH YOUR HEAD FOR A CHANGE.

Harper Lee, from *To Kill a Mockingbird*

Chris Riddell

Anyone who keeps
to the ability
to see beauty
never grows old

- FRANZ KAFKA

Ashley Le Quere

It's lovely to live on a raft. We had the sky up there,
all speckled with stars, and we used to lay on our backs
and look up at them, and discuss about whether they
was made or only just happened
Mark Twain, from *Adventures of Huckleberry Finn*

Eleanor Crow

If you are neutral in situations of injustice, you have
chosen the side of the oppressor. If an elephant has his foot
on the tail of the mouse, and you say that you are neutral,
the mouse will not appreciate your neutrality.
Desmond Tutu

Quentin Blake

Umuntu ngumuntu ngabantu
(A person is a person through other people)
Zulu proverb

David Broadbent

"No one believes more firmly than Comrade Napoleon that all animals are equal. He would be only too happy to let you make your decisions for yourselves. But sometimes you might make the wrong decisions, comrades, and then where should we be?"
George Orwell, from *Animal Farm*

Hannah Rollings

We speak
for the same reason
that
the flowers bloom
that the sun sets
that the fruit ripens
Merle Collins, from 'Because the Dawn Breaks'

Andrea D'Aquino

Those who do not move, do not notice their chains.
Rosa Luxemburg

Decue Wu

For to be free is not merely to cast off one's chains, but to live
in a way that respects and enhances the freedom of others
Nelson Mandela, from *Long Walk to Freedom*

Ellen Surrey

I disapprove of what you say, but I will defend to the death your right to say it

Evelyn Beatrice Hall, from *The Friends of Voltaire*

Tony Husband

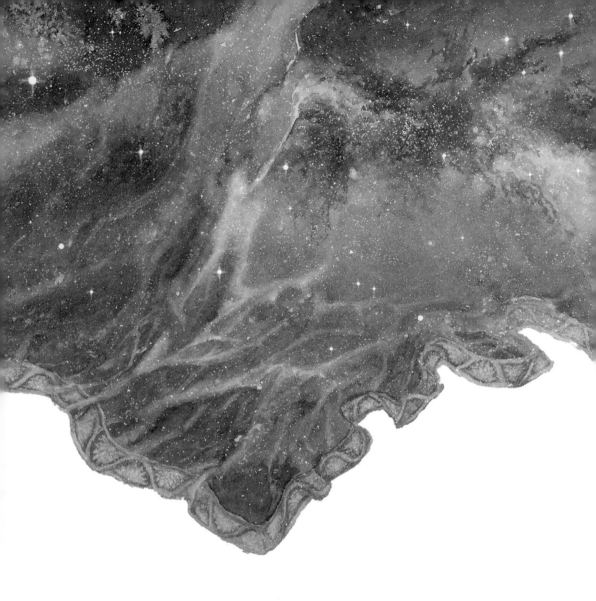

Had I the heavens' embroidered cloths,
Enwrought with golden and silver light,
The blue and the dim and the dark cloths
Of night and light and the half-light,
I would spread the cloths under your feet:
But I, being poor, have only my dreams;
I have spread my dreams under your feet;
Tread softly because you tread on my dreams.
William Butler Yeats, from 'He wishes for the Cloths of Heaven'

Alan Lee

'Thought', **Hannah Rollings**

There is no beauty in the finest cloth if it makes hunger and unhappiness.
Mahatma Gandhi

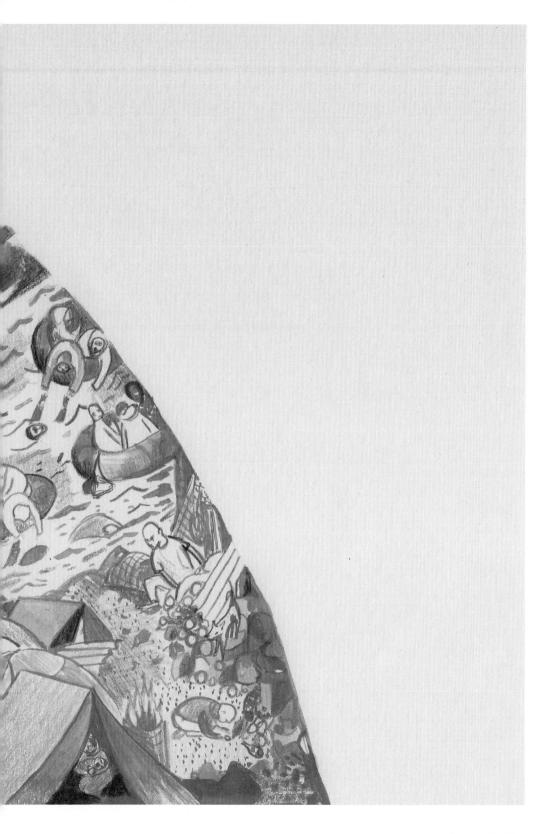

Imogen Rockley

"Differences of habit and language are nothing at all
if our aims are identical and our hearts are open."
J. K. Rowling, from *Harry Potter and the Goblet of Fire*

Jean Jullien

She had not known the weight, until she felt the freedom!
Nathaniel Hawthorne, from *The Scarlet Letter*

Poonam Mistry

When I draw, it is as if a voice is shouting inside me.
Ali Ferzat

Christopher David Ryan

It is through disobedience that progress has been made,
through disobedience and through rebellion.
Oscar Wilde, from 'The Soul of Man under Socialism'

Lizzy Stewart

'Liberty', **Stik**

I
like when
the music happens like this:

Something in His eye grabs hold of a
tambourine in
me,

then I turn and lift a violin in someone else,
and they turn, and this turning
continues;

it has
reached you now. Isn't that
something?

Rūmī, from 'Isn't That Something?'

Raouf Karray

'Family', **Meera Lee Patel**

'Expression', Ashley Le Quere

AND AS I SAW THESE BEAUTIFUL BIRDS CALLING TO EACH OTHER HIGH UP IN THE BRANCHES I REALISED WHAT FREEDOM REALLY MEANT AND HOW RARE IT WAS AND I SAW HOW MUCH WE NEEDED TO SHARE OUR FREEDOM AND I ONLY TRULY BEGAN TO FEEL FREE WHEN I BEGAN TO WANT IT FOR EVERYONE ELSE. THERE'S NO FREEDOM AT ALL IN BEING FREE IF EVERY SINGLE OTHER PERSON ISN'T.

Rob Ryan

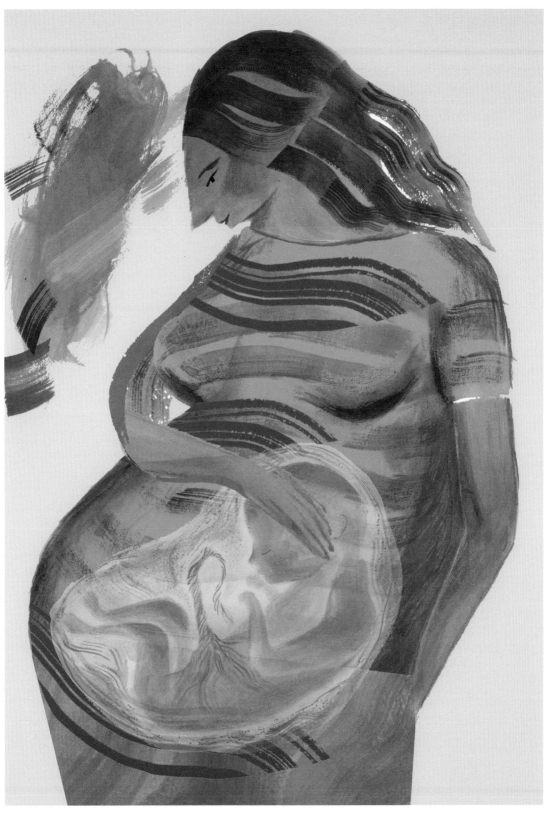

'Hope', Hannah Rollings

Dragonfly catcher,
Where today
have you gone?
Fukuda Chiyo-ni

Sydney Smith

We are made for the sublime and for freedom
Desmond Tutu, from *Freedom*

Owen Davey

"The pen is mightier than the sword."
Edward Bulwer-Lytton, from *Richelieu*

David Broadbent

Freedom
Is a strong seed
Planted
In a great need.

I live here, too.
I want freedom
Just as you.
Langston Hughes, from 'Democracy'

William Grill

Ashley Le Quere

It is better to light a candle than to curse the darkness

Chinese proverb

Keith Negley

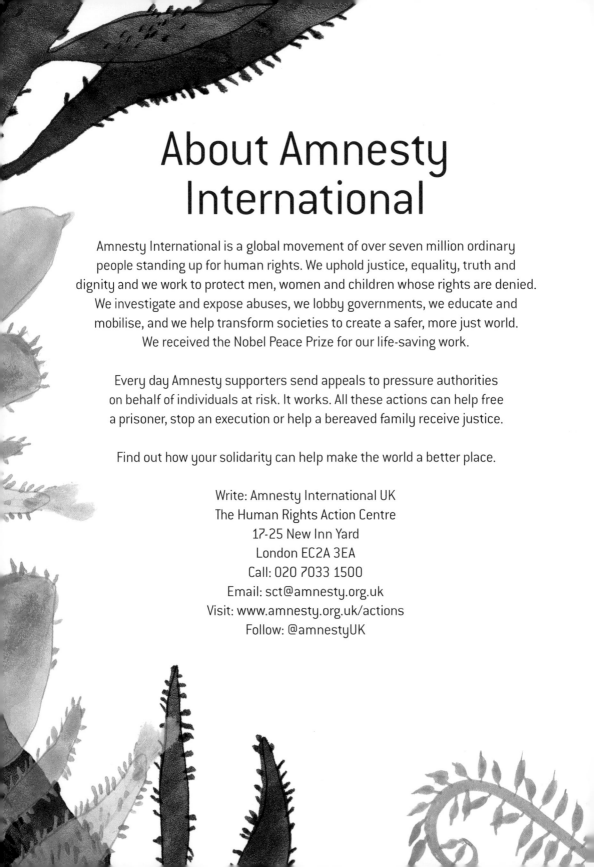

About Amnesty International

Amnesty International is a global movement of over seven million ordinary people standing up for human rights. We uphold justice, equality, truth and dignity and we work to protect men, women and children whose rights are denied. We investigate and expose abuses, we lobby governments, we educate and mobilise, and we help transform societies to create a safer, more just world. We received the Nobel Peace Prize for our life-saving work.

Every day Amnesty supporters send appeals to pressure authorities on behalf of individuals at risk. It works. All these actions can help free a prisoner, stop an execution or help a bereaved family receive justice.

Find out how your solidarity can help make the world a better place.

Write: Amnesty International UK
The Human Rights Action Centre
17-25 New Inn Yard
London EC2A 3EA
Call: 020 7033 1500
Email: sct@amnesty.org.uk
Visit: www.amnesty.org.uk/actions
Follow: @amnestyUK

About Write For Rights

Write for Rights is an annual campaign run by Amnesty where people send messages of hope. In 2016, one of the individuals featured was Native American activist Leonard Peltier, who has been in jail for more than four decades. British fashion designer and activist Dame Vivienne Westwood wrote to him in a gesture of solidarity. This is part of her letter.

"Life is a gift, and I want to repay that by understanding and appreciating the world I live in — it's our duty. My slogan for this is Get A Life: you get out what you put in — you get knowledge. This is freedom, you are in control over your own existence. Understanding the past — not just the past of your own people, but all the people of the world — gives knowledge and knowledge belongs to you.

Every great book is a timeless vision of the world and is as alive today as when it was written. We can be more free by putting ourselves in other people's shoes ..."

Dame Vivienne Westwood

Acknowledgements and permissions

Words

Charlotte Brontë (1816–1855) was an English novelist and poet. *Jane Eyre* was first published in 1847 under the pseudonym Currer Bell.

Edward Bulwer-Lytton (1803–1873) was an English politician, poet and novelist.

Lewis Carroll (1832–1898) was an English writer. His birth name was Charles Lutwidge Dodgson and he is most well-known for his novel, *Alice's Adventures in Wonderland*.
[Extract from 'To Janet Merriman', from *A Selection from the Letters of Lewis Carroll*, 1933]

Fukuda Chiyo-ni (1703–1775) was a Japanese poet, considered to be one of the greatest female hokku poets.

Merle Collins (b. 1950) is a Grenadian poet and short story writer. *Because the Dawn Breaks!*, her first poetry collection, was published in 1985.
[Extract from 'Because the Dawn Breaks', from *Because the Dawn Breaks!: Poems Dedicated to the Grenadian People*, copyright © Merle Collins, 1985]

Ali Ferzat (b. 1951) is a Syrian political cartoonist, living in exile in Kuwait. In 2011 he was awarded the Sakharov Prize for freedom of thought and in 2012 he was named one of the 100 most influential people in the world by *Time* magazine.

Mahatma Gandhi (1869–1948) was a primary leader of India's independence movement. He is internationally respected for his nonviolent principles.

Evelyn Beatrice Hall (1868–1956) was an English writer who wrote under the pseudonym S. G. Tallentyre. She is best known for her biography about Voltaire (1694–1778), who was a French philosopher and author.
[Extract from *The Friends of Voltaire*, copyright © Evelyn Beatrice Hall, 1907]

Nathaniel Hawthorne (1804–1864) was an American novelist and short story writer.

Langston Hughes (1902–1967) was an American poet, social activist, novelist and playwright.
[Extract from 'Democracy' from *The Collected Poems of Langston Hughes* by Langston Hughes, edited by Arnold Rampersad with David Roessel, Associate Editor, copyright © 1994 by the Estate of Langston Hughes. Used by permission of Alfred A. Knopf, an imprint of the Knopf Doubleday Publishing Group, a division of Penguin Random House LLC. All rights reserved.]

Robert G. Ingersoll (1833–1899) was an American politician and orator.

Lyndon B. Johnson (1908–1973) was President of the United States. In 1964, during his administration, he signed the Civil Rights Act into law.

Franz Kafka (1883–1924) was a German-language novelist and short story writer.

Martin Luther King, Jr. (1929–1968) was an American religious leader and civil-rights activist.

D. H. Lawrence (1885–1930) was one of the most influential English authors of the 20th century.
[Extract from 'Bavarian Gentians' from *The Cambridge Edition of The Poems of D. H. Lawrence,* edited by Christopher Pollnitz, © copyright 2013 Cambridge University Press reproduced by permission of Pollinger Ltd (www.pollingerltd.com) on behalf of the Estate of Frieda Lawrence Ravagli.]

Harper Lee (1926–2016) was an American writer, most well known for her novel *To Kill A Mockingbird*.
[Extract from *To Kill A Mockingbird* by Harper Lee, published by J. B. Lippincott & Co (Copyright © Harper Lee, 1960)]

Rosa Luxemburg (1871–1919) was a Polish-born German revolutionary.

Nelson Mandela (1918–2013) was a black nationalist and the first black president of South Africa.
[Extract from *Long Walk to Freedom* by Nelson Mandela (Copyright © Nelson Mandela, 1995)]

Bob Marley (1945–1981) was a Jamaican singer-songwriter.
[Extract from 'Get Up, Stand Up', copyright © Bob Marley and the Wailers, 1973]

Martin Niemöller (1892–1984) was a German theologian and pastor.

George Orwell (1903–1950) was an English author.
[Extract from *Animal Farm* by George Orwell (Copyright © George Orwell, 1945). Reprinted by permission of Bill Hamilton as the Literary Executor of the Estate of the Late Sonia Brownell Orwell.]

J. K. Rowling (b. 1965) is an English novelist, screenwriter and film producer, best known as the author of the Harry Potter fantasy series.
[Extract from *Harry Potter and the Goblet of Fire* by J. K. Rowling (Copyright © J. K. Rowling, 2000)]

Rūmī (1207–1273) was a Sufi mystic and poet.

William Shakespeare (1564–1616) was an English poet and playwright.

Desmond Tutu (b. 1931) is a South African Anglican cleric who received the Nobel Prize for Peace for his role in the opposition to apartheid.

Mark Twain (1835–1910) was an American writer. His works include the classic novels *The Adventures of Tom Sawyer* and *Adventures of Huckleberry Finn*. His real name was Samuel Langhorne Clemens but he wrote under the pseudonym Mark Twain.

Umuntu ngumuntu ngabantu is a Zulu proverb which means a person is only a person through other people. It's a version of a saying that is widely echoed in Africa. The concept expresses the essence of 'ubuntu', a southern African philosophy, which roughly translates as 'humanness', and has been cited frequently by Nelson Mandela and Desmond Tutu in recent decades. As Desmond Tutu said, "You can't be human all by yourself".

Earl Warren (1891–1974) was an American jurist and the 14th chief justice of the United States between 1953 and 1969.

Vivienne Westwood (b. 1941) is an English fashion designer and activist whose work has influenced millions of people around the world.

Oscar Wilde (1854–1900) was an Irish poet, dramatist and author, well known for his play *The Importance of Being Earnest* (1895) and his only novel, *The Picture of Dorian Gray* (1891).

William Butler Yeats (1865–1939) was an Irish author and poet who received the Nobel Prize for Literature in 1923.

Malala Yousafzai (b. 1997) is a Pakistani activist. Yousafzai and Kailash Satyarthi were jointly awarded the Nobel Prize for Peace in 2014, for their efforts on behalf of children's rights.
[Extract reproduced with permission of Curtis Brown Group Ltd, London on behalf of Malala Yousafzai. Copyright © Malala Yousafzai 2013. Taken from Malala Yousafzai's Speech to the United Nations.]

Artists

Quentin Blake was born in Sidcup in 1932 and has drawn ever since he can remember. His books have won numerous prizes and awards and he received a knighthood for 'services to illustration' in the New Year's Honours for 2013, and became an Honorary Freeman of the City of London in 2015.

David Broadbent has created many illustrations for many varied companies. He grew up in Yorkshire in the north of England, and currently resides in Brighton on the south coast, living there with two children, a wife and a whippet. He enjoys cycling, walking and cake.

Mia Charro (www.miacharro.com) was born in Amorebieta, a beautiful town in Vizcaya in the north of Spain. She has worked in illustration and graphic design for 16 years. Her inspiration is Mother Nature, yoga, meditation and ancient wisdom.

Christopher Corr is a British artist who studied at the Royal College of Art. His gouache illustrations are inspired by his round-the-world travels, and his vibrant picture books include *Don't Spill the Milk*, *Deep in the Woods* and *A Year Full of Stories*.

Eleanor Crow is a versatile illustrator and designer, who has created numerous book jackets for Random House, the Folio Society and Faber & Faber. Her illustration work has been commissioned internationally and in the UK. She trained at Edinburgh and Central Saint Martins, and lives in London.

Andrea D'Aquino is an illustrator whose work has been published internationally. Her books are *Once Upon a Piece of Paper*, an illustrated book about collage, and a very modern and quirky version of the classic *Alice's Adventures in Wonderland*, both published by Quarto.

Owen Davey is an award-winning illustrator from the UK. He illustrates the immensely popular puzzle app TwoDots, and has picture books published on every continent except Antarctica. Other clients include Facebook, Google, Sony and *The New York Times*.

Shane W. Evans is the illustrator of many picture books for children and has won numerous awards. He has exhibited his art all over the world and lives in Kansas City where he runs Dream Studio, a community art space. Find out more at www.dreamstudio777.com.

William Grill is a London-based illustrator who has worked for a variety of clients such as *The New York Times*, Harrods and Shelter. His first book, *Shackleton's Journey,* won the 2015 Kate Greenaway award and has been translated into 14 languages.

Natalie Hughes has a bright, graphic style with a strong use of colour and atmosphere. Drawn to telling simple yet meaningful stories, Natalie is inspired by travel, 80's films, dream-like landscapes, and strange plants and creatures. Based in Yorkshire, Natalie works with a range of international clients across publishing and editorial.

Tony Husband has been a full-time cartoonist since 1984. His cartoons have appeared in many newspapers, magazines, books and websites, and in several TV and theatrical productions. He has won more than 15 major awards including the Pont Award for depicting the British way of life.

Frances Ives completed her MA in Illustration from University of the Arts London, and now works from her home studio. Frances works primarily in watercolour and ink, but her illustrations involve a variety of media, which is often digitally composed.

Jean Jullien is a French graphic artist currently living in London and Los Angeles. Originally hailing from Nantes, Jean completed a graphic design degree in Quimper before moving to London, where he graduated from Central Saint Martins in 2008 and the Royal College of Art in 2010. His practice ranges from illustration to photography, video, costumes, installations, books, posters and clothing. Jean's first monograph, *Modern Life,* was published by teNeues in October 2016.

Raouf Karray is a Palestinian illustrator and graphic artist who is Professor of Visual Communication and Graphic Arts at the University of Sfax in Tunisia. His books are published in France, Italy and Tunisia and he is a recipient of the Noma Concours for Picture Book Illustrations Award.

Alan Lee is a Dartmoor-based illustrator of books of fantasy and mythology, including many by J. R. R. Tolkien. He also works in film and received an Academy Award for his design work on *The Lord of the Rings – The Return of the King*. Alan's illustration in this book depicts Maud Gonne, William Butler Yeats' muse. The birds, which figure prominently in Yeats' poetry, are also a reference to the pet birds that always accompanied her.

Poonam Mistry is a freelance illustrator living in the UK. Her work is influenced by her Indian roots and celebrates her love of folklore and traditional art with the use of patterns and intricate details.

Keith Negley is a frequent contributor to *The New York Times* and *The New Yorker*, as well as many other national magazines and newspapers. His work has appeared on everything from skateboard decks to children's books, and he's won many awards and accolades for his illustrations.

Meera Lee Patel is a self-taught artist and author who creates work that encourages others to connect with themselves, each other, and the world around them. She is the author of the best-selling journal, *Start Where You Are*. She lives and works in Brooklyn, New York, and can be found online at: www.meeralee.com. She believes that all change starts from within.

Ashley Le Quere is an illustrator, pattern designer and brush lettering lover currently living in London. She has been illustrating books and designing for over seven years, along with finding a passion for pattern and brush lettering along the way!

Chris Riddell is a prolific writer and illustrator. He is known especially for his distinctive line drawings with their clever caricature and fascinating detail. He was the Waterstones' Children's Laureate 2015–2017, and has won the prestigious CILIP Kate Greenaway Medal three times. In addition to his children's books, Chis is a renowned political cartoonist whose work appears in *The Observer*, *The Literary Review* and *The New Statesman*.

Imogen Rockley was born in Berkshire and studied at Chelsea School of Art and then Falmouth University. She now lives and works in Brighton as an illustrator, where she can observe and draw her favourite things; people and the sea.

Hannah Rollings is the illustrator of *An Artist Once Said: An Inspiration Book for Artists*, and *Doodle a Poodle* and *Colour a Cat*, cataloging over 60 breeds with handy tips for budding artistic animal lovers.

Christopher David Ryan (CDR) makes art constantly, sometimes quite literally covering the walls with the narrative of his hyperactive imagination. His characters embrace, they reach out to one another, and they reflect the small truths of daily life; sometimes with irony but never with sarcasm. A cosmic enthusiast and deep thinker, CDR literally tries to make the world better through art — promoting peace and love in vibrant colour and without self-censure.

Rob Ryan has exhibited widely across the UK and internationally, and has written and illustrated several books. His work often consists of whimsical figures paired with sentimental, grave, honest and occasionally humorous pieces of writing, which he admits are autobiographical.

Eleanor Shakespeare is a photomontage illustrator living and working in London. She has had a number of books published for children and adults, as well as working with editorial clients worldwide. Her work combines found images with colour, texture and hand-drawn type. Eleanor runs creative workshops for young people and in her spare time enjoys running, playing the piano and exploring London.

David Shrigley is an artist best known for his mordantly humorous cartoons. Sometimes considered an outsider in the art world, Shrigley is known for making flat compositions that take on the inconsequential, the bizarre, and the disquieting elements of everyday life. Like the musings of a very wise child displaying the wit and humour of a seasoned observer of the adult world, his drawings feature crossed-out words, scribbled, uneven lines, and darkly funny aphorisms about the world.

Sydney Smith is a Canadian illustrator of children's books. He was awarded the 2015 Governor General's Award For Illustrated Children's Books for *Sidewalk Flowers*, a wordless picture book, which he illustrated with author JonArno Lawson.

Lizzy Stewart is an award-winning illustrator and artist currently based in London. She writes and draws picture books as well as being an Associate Lecturer at Goldsmiths College.

Stik started painting simple line drawings around Hackney during a period of homelessness in the early 2000s. Over a decade, these 'unofficial', socially conscious artworks evolved and started to illustrate the lives of a community facing gentrification and social change. Stik is now known for his ground-breaking initiatives in support of the homeless, the NHS and the LGBTQ+ community. These epic murals are now found from New York to Tokyo documenting the humanitarian struggle of those communities. In 2014 Stik produced the tallest mural in Britain 'Big Mother', highlighting the need for social housing. He still lives and works in Hackney.

Ellen Surrey is a Los Angeles based illustrator and designer. Her primary sources of inspiration come from old Hollywood, mid-century design, and vintage treasures. She enjoys finding the beauty in the past and incorporating it into something contemporary.

Wen Dee Tan graduated in 2014 with a Masters in Children's Book Illustration from Cambridge School of Art, UK. Her debut picture book, *Lili,* was longlisted for the Kate Greenaway Children's Book Award 2016 and shortlisted for the Klaus Flugge Prize 2016. Wen Dee loves to draw and believes good stories are those that appeal to all ages.

Decue Wu is a graphic artist, illustrator and designer, originally from China, and in 2012 she moved to the USA to pursue her art study and career. She focuses on fashion and lifestyle, editorial, pattern, picture books and other visual arts. Her work has been featured in several publications and exhibited around the world.